Healthy Choices

Drinks

Sharon Dalgleish

Smart Apple Media

Smart Apple Media
2140 Howard Drive West
North Mankato
Minnesota 56003

First published in 2006 by
MACMILLAN EDUCATION AUSTRALIA PTY LTD
627 Chapel Street, South Yarra, Australia 3141

Visit our Web site at www.macmillan.com.au

Associated companies and representatives throughout the world.

Library of Congress Cataloging-in-Publication Data

Dalgleish, Sharon.
    Drinks / by Sharon Dalgleish.
        p. cm. — (Healthy choices)
    Includes index.
    ISBN-13: 978-1-58340-745-5
    1. Nutrition--Juvenile literature. 2. Beverages--Juvenile literature. I. Title.

RA784.D335 2006
613.2—dc22

2005057883

Edited by Helen Bethune Moore
Text and cover design by Christine Deering
Page layout by Domenic Lauricella
Photo research by Legend Images
Illustrations by Paul Konye

Printed in USA

Acknowledgments
The author and the publisher are grateful to the following for permission to reproduce copyright material:

Front cover: Girls drinking from water fountain, courtesy of Getty Images/Taxi.

Australian Picture Library/Phil Schermeister/CORBIS, p. 8; Banana Stock, p. 24; Brand X Pictures, pp. 12 (centre left, bottom right & bottom left), 14 (top), 17 (centre), 20 (left & centre), 21 (centre top & left), 27 (top); Corbis Digital Stock, pp. 12 (top right & top left), 20 (right), 25 (left); Digital Vision, pp. 17 (left), 21 (centre bottom); Bill Thomas/Imagen, p. 9; iStockphoto.com, pp. 1, 4 (left), 11 (centre), 13, 14 (bottom), 15, 21 (top right), 27 (bottom); MEA Photo, pp. 3, 10, 11 (left & right), 17 (right), 19, 26; Photodisc, pp. 7, 12 (bottom centre), 22, 25 (centre); Photolibrary RF, p. 25 (right); Photolibrary/Foodpix, p. 16; Photolibrary/Photonica Inc, p. 18; Photolibrary/Plainpicture Gmbh & Co. Kg , pp. 4 (centre), 30; Photolibrary/Reso E.E.I.G, p. 4 (right).

While every care has been taken to trace and acknowledge copyright, the publisher tenders their apologies for any accidental infringement where copyright has proved untraceable. Where the attempt has been unsuccessful, the publisher welcomes information that would redress the situation.

Contents

Healthy, fit, and happy

To be healthy, fit, and happy your body needs:

- a good mix of foods

- plenty of clean drinking water

- a **balance** of activity and rest

water

activity

A good mix of foods, water, rest, and play all help to make you healthy.

mix of foods

Drinks

Just like the food you eat, your body **digests** the **fluids** you drink. When you are thirsty, the food group pyramid can help you make healthy drink choices.

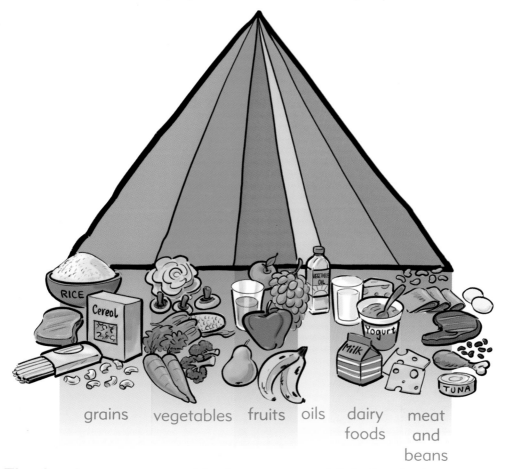

grains   vegetables   fruits   oils   dairy foods   meat and beans

The food group pyramid shows you which foods to eat most for a healthy, balanced diet.

Why make healthy choices?

Making healthy drink choices is important. Your body loses fluid every day. You lose fluid through your skin, when you go to the bathroom, and when you breathe. You need to replace this fluid.

How much should you drink to be healthy?	
Age	**Ounces of fluid per day**
5 to 8 years	28 ounces = 4 to 5 glasses
9 to 12 years	40 ounces = 6 to 7 glasses
adult	56 ounces = 8 to 9 glasses

When you **exercise** and sweat, your body loses fluid. Your body can lose fluid faster than you notice being thirsty. Have a drink, even if you do not feel thirsty.

You need to drink before, during, and after exercise.

Water

Water is the most important **nutrient** of all. Water is the main **ingredient** in all the fluids inside your body, even your blood. Water is the healthiest drink choice.

It is important to drink water when you are out hiking.

Plain water is best because nothing is added to it.
It is a good idea to have your own water bottle.
Fill it up and always take it with you.

Wash your bottle
often in warm,
soapy water,
and then rinse it
in fresh water.

Make water more special

Put some iced water on the dinner table each night. Make it special by floating slices of lemon, lime, or orange in the container.

Add some mint to the water for extra flavor.

Make water more interesting by adding just a dash of pure fruit juice to a glass or jug. Experiment to see the different colors you can make using different juices.

orange juice

grape juice

Just a dash of orange or grape juice will lightly color water.

Juice

Fruits and vegetables have a lot of water in them. Drinking fruit or vegetable juice is one way to replace the fluid your body loses.

Fruits   **Vegetables**

bananas

carrots

watermelon

pineapple   oranges   celery

Whole fruits and vegetables contain **fiber** that juice does not have. Eating whole fruits and vegetables is healthier than having them as juice. However, juice is also a healthy choice.

A glass of orange juice with your cereal is a great way to start the day.

13

Make juicy ice cubes

Ask a parent or teacher for help.

It is fun to make ice cubes with fruit juice. Add them to plain water. For a taste explosion, add them to fresh juice made from a different fruit.

What you need
- watermelon
- an ice-cube tray
- a blender

What to do
1 **Blend watermelon flesh until smooth.**
2 **Pour into an ice-cube tray and freeze.**
3 **Tip out the ice cubes.**
4 **Store in a plastic bag in the freezer until you need them.**

Make orange squeezy

Ask a parent or teacher for help.

Orange juice is easy to make and it is also full of healthy **vitamin C**.

Serves 1

What you need

- 2 oranges
- 3 ice cubes (made with water or juice)
- a knife
- a citrus juicer
- a glass

What to do

1 **Cut the oranges in half.**

2 **Place one half on a citrus juicer, cut side down, and push. As you push, give the orange a twist.**

3 **Keep pushing and twisting until you have squeezed out all the juice. Repeat with the other halves.**

4 **Add ice cubes to a glass and then pour juice over them.**

Make watermelon freeze

Ask a parent
or teacher
for help.

This juice is made in a blender so you will get all the fiber from the fruit too.

Serves 2

What you need

- 4 thick slices of watermelon
- 2 tablespoons of lemon juice
- 16 ice cubes
- a knife
- a blender
- 2 tall glasses

What to do

1 **Roughly chop the watermelon flesh.**

2 **Place it in a blender and add the lemon juice and ice cubes.**

3 **Blend until smooth.**

4 **Serve in tall glasses.**

Make pink banana crush

Ask a parent or teacher for help.

It can be lots of fun to experiment and make up your own juice recipe.

Serves 1

What you need

- 1 banana, peeled and frozen
- a handful of strawberries, frozen
- a dash of orange juice
- a blender
- a tall glass

orange juice

What to do

1 **Place all ingredients in a blender.**
2 **Blend until smooth.**
3 **Serve in a tall glass.**
4 **Enjoy!**

Milk

Milk group foods contain **calcium**. Calcium helps your bones and teeth grow strong and healthy. Your bones and teeth are alive and need healthy food, too.

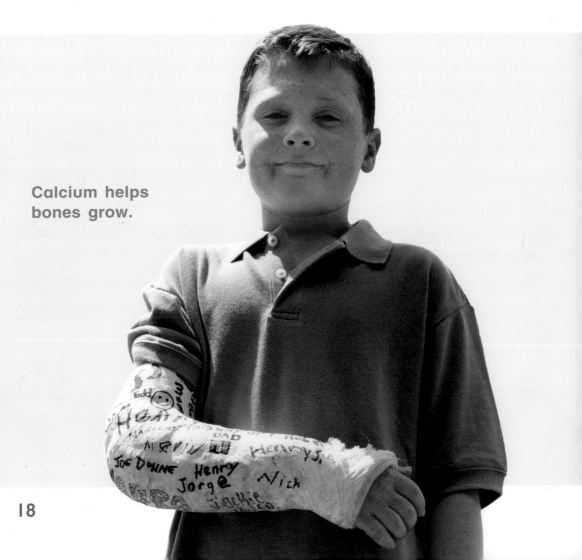

Calcium helps bones grow.

You need twice as much calcium as an adult does. Your bones and teeth are still growing. By the time you are an adult, you will have 28 teeth.

You need to drink about 3 glasses or 24 ounces (750 milliliters) of milk each day.

Make a milk shake

Ask a parent or teacher for help.

In this recipe, you could swap the kiwi for a banana, half a cup of blueberries or strawberries, or chunks of peach.

Serves 1

What you need
- 1 kiwi
- 1 cup low-fat milk
- a blender
- a tall glass

What to do

1 **Peel the kiwi and chop it roughly.**

2 **Place in blender and add the milk.**

3 **Blend until smooth and frothy.**

4 **Serve in a tall glass.**

Make an egg flip

Ask a parent
or teacher
for help.

This is a breakfast you can drink!

Serves 1

What you need

- ½ cup low-fat milk
- ½ cup plain low-fat yogurt
- 1 banana, peeled
- 1 teaspoon honey
- 1 egg
- blender
- tall glass

What to do

1 **Place milk, yogurt, banana and honey in the blender.**

2 **Break the egg into the blender.**

3 **Blend until smooth and frothy.**

4 **Pour into a tall glass.**

low-fat
yogurt

honey

21

Sports and energy drinks

Some drinks are sold as "sports" or "energy" drinks. These are not healthy choices for you. Sports drinks contain lots of sugar and salt. Energy drinks contain sugar and **caffeine**.

An energy drink has as much caffeine as a cup of coffee.

When you play sport or need energy, eat an orange and drink plain water. You should drink water before, during, and after exercise.

Water and exercise	
When	**How much?**
1 to 2 hours before exercise	drink about 1½ cups of water
10 to 15 minutes before exercise	drink about 1 cup of water
during exercise	drink about ½ cup water every 15 minutes
after exercise	drink 1 or 2 cups of water, more if it is a very hot day

Sodas

Sodas contain sugar and **acid** that attack your teeth. If the attacks keep happening, they can cause holes in your teeth.

If you drink soda, use a straw to keep the sugar and acid away from your teeth.

Make lemon cooler

You can make your own sparkling drinks when you are having a party.

Serves 2

What you need

- 2 lemons
- 16 ounces (500 milliliters) sparkling mineral water
- 6 ice cubes
- 4 to 6 fresh mint leaves
- a jug
- a stirring spoon

What to do

1 **Squeeze the juice from the lemons.**
2 **Pour the juice into a jug.**
3 **Add the mineral water, ice cubes, and mint leaves.**
4 **Stir it all together.**

Popsicles

You can make your own healthy popsicles. Mix up any juice or milk shake recipe. Pour the mixture into a mold and freeze overnight, or for at least six hours.

These popsicle molds have straws as well as handles.

26

Make berry yogurt popsicles

These popsicles are very good for your bones.
They contain yogurt for added calcium.

Serves 3

What you need

- 1½ cups plain low-fat yogurt
- 1 cup frozen berries, such as strawberries or blueberries
- 1 tablespoon honey
- a bowl
- popsicle molds
- a spoon

What to do

1 **Mix all ingredients in a bowl.**
2 **Spoon into popsicle molds.**
3 **Press on lids.**
4 **Freeze overnight.**

blueberries

low-fat
yogurt

Make three-fruit popsicles

These popsicles are made with three fruits that are full of **vitamin C**.

Serves 3 to 6

What you need

- 15 ounce (425 gram) can peaches
- ½ cup orange juice
- 1 passion fruit

- a strainer
- a blender
- popsicle molds
- a spoon

What to do

1 **Strain peaches and place them in blender.**

2 **Add orange juice and blend until smooth.**

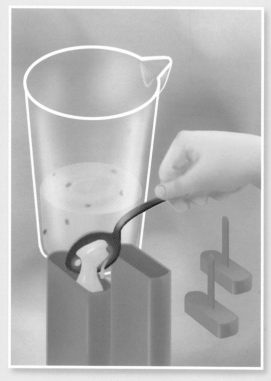

3 Cut passion fruit in half. Scoop out the pulp and add pulp to blender. Blend just enough to mix it in.

4 Spoon into popsicle molds. Press on lids and freeze overnight.

Healthy choices for life

Making healthy choices in everything you do will help you to be fit, happy, and healthy.

Life is fun when you make healthy choices.

Glossary

acid	a substance that can eat away at minerals
balance	an equal amount of different things
caffeine	a substance found in coffee and sports drinks
calcium	a mineral found in food that helps build strong bones
digests	breaks down food and fluids inside the body
exercise	use your body to make it strong and healthy
fiber	found in plant foods, and helps your body break down food
fluids	liquids
ingredient	one of the parts of a mixture
nutrient	healthy substance found in food, such as a vitamin or mineral
vitamin C	a nutrient that helps fight colds and infections

Index